Dyslexia

ANN O. SQUIRE

Children's Press®
An Imprint of Scholastic Inc.

Boyle County Public Library

Content Consultant
Phyllis Meadows, PhD, MSN, RN
Associate Dean for Practice, Clinical Professor, Health Management and Policy
University of Michigan, Ann Arbor, Michigan

Library of Congress Cataloging-in-Publication Data
Names: Squire, Ann, author.
Title: Dyslexia / by Ann O. Squire.
Other titles: True book.
Description: New York, NY : Children's Press, an imprint of Scholastic Inc., [2017] | Series: A true
  book | Includes bibliographical references and index.
Identifiers: LCCN 2015048542| ISBN 9780531228432 (library binding) | ISBN 9780531233276 (pbk.)
Subjects: LCSH: Dyslexia—Juvenile literature. | Language disorders—Juvenile literature.
Classification: LCC RC394.W6 S68 2017 | DDC 616.85/53—dc23
LC record available at http://lccn.loc.gov/2015048542

© 2017 Scholastic Inc.
All rights reserved. Published in 2017 by Children's Press, an imprint of Scholastic Inc.
Printed in China 62
SCHOLASTIC, CHILDREN'S PRESS, A TRUE BOOK™, and associated logos are trademarks and/or
registered trademarks of Scholastic Inc.
1 2 3 4 5 6 7 8 9 10 R 26 25 24 23 22 21 20 19 18 17

Front cover: A frustrated girl at a chalkboard
Back cover: A child holding up letters

Find the Truth!

Everything you are about to read is true *except* for one of the sentences on this page.

Which one is **TRUE**?

T or F Many successful people have suffered from dyslexia.

T or F There are a number of medicines that are used to treat dyslexia.

Find the answers in this book.

3

Contents

THE **BIG** TRUTH!

Dyslexia Didn't Stop Them!

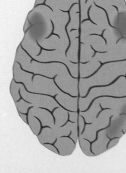

Activity in a
dyslexic brain

Dyslexia can make it tough to do well in school.

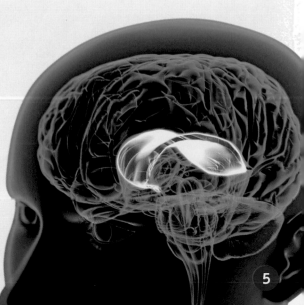

The human brain, with the corpus callosum highlighted in orange

CHAPTER 1

What Can It Be?

Joey's mom was worried. She had just received a call from his second-grade teacher. The teacher was concerned about Joey's reading. Joey read much more slowly than the other students. He often seemed frustrated and upset when he tried to read. The other kids were learning to sound out unfamiliar words and then recognize them by sight, but Joey was struggling.

Matching written letters with the sounds they stand for is difficult for people with dyslexia.

Word Problems

Joey's mom wasn't surprised to hear what the teacher said. Joey was very bright, but he had always had trouble with words. As a baby, he had begun talking much later than his two older sisters. He also had a hard time learning new words. The family sometimes listened to audio books, and Joey was always interested in the stories. But he never wanted to try reading them himself.

Siblings might start talking and reading at very different ages.

Difficulty reading can lead kids to believe they are not as smart as their classmates.

That evening, Joey's mom and dad asked their son about school.

"I hate it!" Joey replied. "Especially reading. I read so much slower than everybody else. Sometimes the words and letters look all jumbled up. Everybody thinks I'm dumb." Then he added, "Maybe I am. Reading seems so easy for everyone else, but it's so hard for me."

Teachers are often the first to notice when a child has a learning disability.

Joey's parents realized that they needed to do something. They wanted their son to enjoy school, not hate it. The next day, Joey's mom called the teacher to ask for her advice. What did she think Joey's problem was? Did she have any suggestions for fixing it? The teacher replied that she suspected Joey had a **learning disability** called dyslexia.

Kids with dyslexia have trouble matching written letters with the sounds they stand for. This affects reading speed and accuracy. It also makes it harder for them to understand and remember what they read. People with dyslexia often have trouble spelling, too. Along with other issues, these problems make it very difficult for a child to read. Joey's teacher suggested that he be tested for the **disorder**.

Students who have trouble reading are also likely to have difficulty with spelling and other writing skills.

CHAPTER 2

Making a Diagnosis

The first step was a visit to Joey's doctor. He performed a physical exam and took a complete health history. Because Joey said that written words sometimes looked jumbled and hard to see, the doctor tested his vision. He also tested Joey's hearing. The doctor said Joey had no physical problems that could explain his difficulties with reading. He recommended visiting a learning disabilities specialist.

Vision and hearing problems do not cause dyslexia.

A learning disabilities specialist can learn a lot about a patient just by talking with him or her.

The Testing Process

The specialist began the appointment by talking with Joey. She asked him about his favorite school subjects and his least favorite ones. It was a relaxed afternoon, but as they were chatting, the specialist was paying close attention to Joey's speech. People with dyslexia sometimes pause when talking or take a long time to say something. They may also make mistakes with words and have a hard time telling a story.

The specialist asked Joey's parents some questions. They explained that he had been late to start talking and that he had used "baby talk" for several years. They also reported that he had had trouble remembering the letters in his name. He often held books upside down. He paid more attention to the pictures than the words, and he sometimes forgot that words are read left to right.

Some children show more interest than others in books when they are young.

After they had talked for a while, the specialist said that she wanted to give Joey a few tests. She didn't want him to worry about doing well. The purpose of the tests was to give her information that would help her understand his reading problem. There are many tests that can be used to **diagnose** dyslexia. These include reading tests, language and vocabulary tests, hearing-based tests, and general intelligence tests.

Dyslexia makes it difficult to recognize letters strung together into words. Tests help check for this.

Sounding out each word individually makes it hard to understand the meaning of a whole sentence.

The test results indicated that Joey did have a reading disability. When he tried to read a word, he had trouble matching the printed letters on the page with the **phonemes** that made up the words. Struggling with each word caused Joey to read very slowly, and he did not remember much of what he had read. The good news was that Joey's intelligence was well above normal.

CHAPTER 3

Explaining the Disability

Based on her conversations with Joey and his parents, along with the results of the tests, the specialist concluded that Joey definitely suffered from dyslexia. Joey was relieved that his problem had a name and that he was not lazy or unintelligent. His parents were relieved, too, but also concerned. What exactly was dyslexia? Could it be treated? Would Joey always have it? How would it affect his future?

Dyslexia is a lifelong condition, but people can learn to succeed in spite of it.

The Dyslexic Brain

The learning specialist explained that dyslexia has nothing to do with how intelligent a person is or how hard he or she works. It is a **neurobiological** disorder. This means a dyslexic person's brain is "wired" a bit differently from that of a person without the disorder. On the wall of the office was a drawing of a human brain. The specialist used it to explain what she meant.

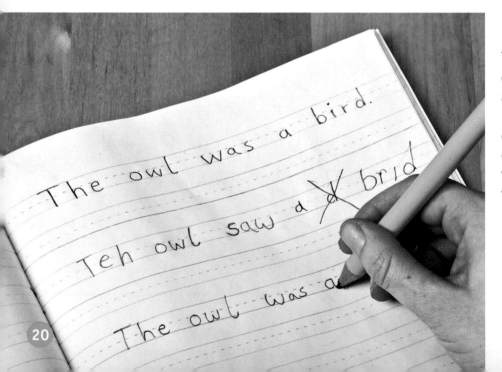

The brains of dyslexic people and non-dyslexic people function differently, especially when working with words and language.

The right side of the brain is more active in a dyslexic person than it is in a non-dyslexic person.

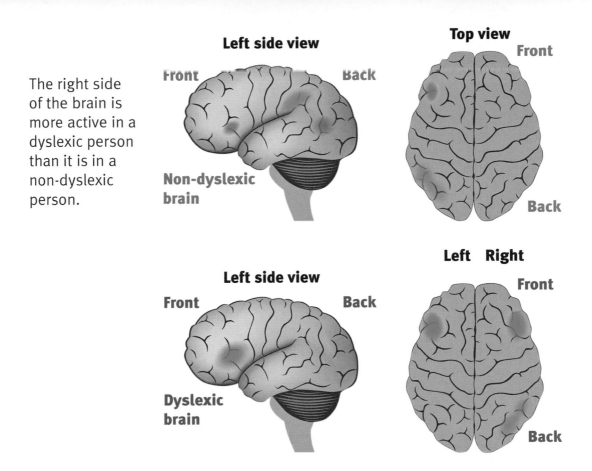

Left side view

Front   Back

Non-dyslexic brain

Top view

Front

Back

Left side view

Front   Back

Dyslexic brain

Left   Right

Front

Back

The brain is divided into two **hemispheres**. Each hemisphere has a different job. The left hemisphere is in charge of language, math, and logic. The right hemisphere handles **spatial** activities, music, and art. Most people use both hemispheres for different tasks. But people with dyslexia seem to rely on the right hemisphere more than the left.

How can we see what's going on in someone's brain? An MRI is a test that uses a magnetic field and radio waves to create detailed images of the organs and tissues inside the body. MRIs have been used to compare the brains of dyslexics to those of non-dyslexics. Doctors also use PET scans to examine dyslexic patients. PET scans let doctors see how blood flows to different areas of the body.

MRI stands for "magnetic resonance imaging," and PET stands for "positron emission tomography."

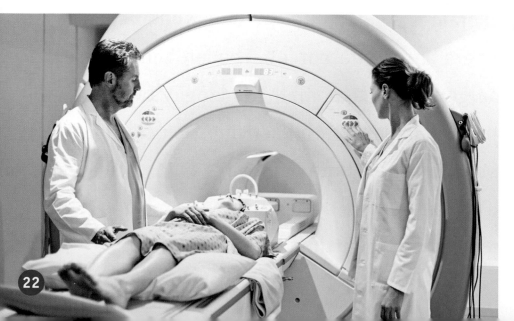

A patient's head is scanned by a large MRI machine.

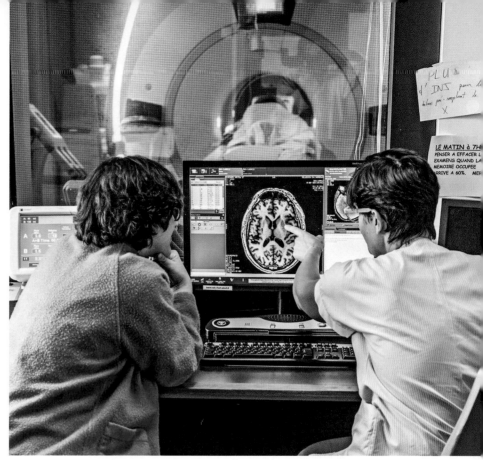

MRIs have revealed that areas in the left hemisphere that are associated with language and reading look very different in the brains of people with dyslexia. There may also be differences in other parts of the brain. Some scientists believe that the left-brain areas related to reading are not developed as well in dyslexic people.

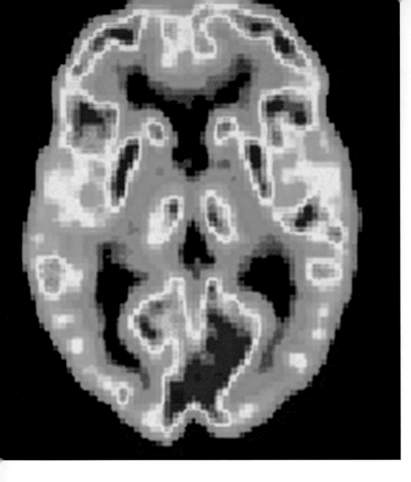

A PET scan shows the way blood moves through a non-dyslexic brain.

PET scans have been used to compare blood flow to different parts of the brain when people are performing various tasks. When non-dyslexics are asked to read and sound out words, an area on the left side of their brain "lights up" as blood flows to that area. When people with dyslexia are given the same task, the language area does not light up.

The Corpus Callosum

The left and right hemispheres of the brain have different specialties, but they are not completely separate. A band of tissue called the **corpus callosum** is a bridge between the two hemispheres. It transfers information from one side to the other. Studies have shown that the corpus callosum is different in dyslexics and non-dyslexics. Some researchers believe that slow transfer between the hemispheres may contribute to dyslexia.

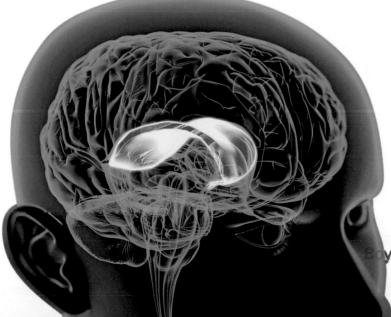

The corpus callosum, shown here in orange, connects the two hemispheres of the brain.

A Family Affair

Many studies have shown that dyslexia runs in families. One study found that dyslexics were more than three times as likely to have a parent, brother, or sister with the disorder than non-dyslexics were. Scientists are now working to pinpoint the **genes** that may cause dyslexia. They hope that learning more about the causes of dyslexia will help them find effective treatments and maybe even a cure.

Analyzing the genes of people with dyslexia has helped scientists begin to learn about the disability's possible causes.

A Lifelong Disorder

Dyslexia is a lifelong disorder. It will not go away on its own, and dyslexics will not grow out of it. The key to living with dyslexia is for people to find effective treatments that allow them to improve their reading skills and learn well despite their disability. The fact that many people have overcome their dyslexia and gone on to have happy and successful lives shows that it can be done!

Dyslexia Didn't Stop Them!

If you have been diagnosed with dyslexia, it can be tempting to think that you will never be a good reader. You might worry that you will not do well in school or be able to go to college. You can put those worries aside! Many famous people have overcome dyslexia and accomplished incredible things. Some even credit their disability with giving them the skills to build a successful life.

Steven Spielberg is the director behind *Jurassic Park*, *E.T.*, the Indiana Jones series, and many other classic movies. As a kid, he did poorly in school. His teachers often called him "lazy." It was not until he was an adult that he found out he has dyslexia. Making films helped Spielberg find a way to express himself that didn't depend heavily on words.

Steven Spielberg

Whoopi Goldberg

Keira Knightley

Many other creative people also suffer from dyslexia, including comedian Whoopi Goldberg, and actors Channing Tatum and Keira Knightley. Apple co-founder Steve Jobs, inventors Alexander Graham Bell and Thomas Edison, and physicist Albert Einstein also struggled with it.

Channing Tatum

Steve Jobs

Being able to identify the different sounds in each word is an important part of overcoming dyslexia.

CHAPTER 4

Treating Dyslexia

Though dyslexia is a lifelong condition, there are many treatments that can help people overcome the disorder. One of the most common treatments focuses on helping dyslexics learn which sounds make up words. For example, the word *cat* is made up of three sounds: "cuh," "a," and "tuh." This ability to distinguish between sounds is called **phonemic awareness**.

Dyslexia affects 10 to 15 percent of Americans.

Dyslexics work closely with therapists and teachers to improve their reading and writing skills.

Words and Sounds

The next step is teaching the dyslexic person to combine letters and phonemes to create words and then use those words in complex sentences. Treatment also focuses on reading practice to help the person recognize words more quickly and accurately. Because many dyslexics have trouble remembering and understanding what they have read, treatment includes strategies to help them monitor their own understanding.

Using Several Senses

Perhaps because they rely more on the right side of the brain, many dyslexic people are especially creative and artistic. It is often easier for them to learn if they use several senses at once. An example of this approach would be to read a letter, say its name and its sound, and write it on a piece of paper, all at the same time. This helps the dyslexic person link written letters or words with their sounds or meanings.

Writing letters over and over while saying them aloud makes it easier for dyslexic people to make a connection between written and spoken language.

A Matter of Time

In addition to having sessions with learning or reading specialists, many kids with dyslexia find that they need extra time to complete tests and homework. At schools, specialists and teachers work together to help dyslexic students. They make sure these students have every opportunity to keep up with other kids and avoid falling behind.

Timeline of Dyslexia Discovery

1887

The word *dyslexia* is first used to describe difficulties with learning to read.

1896

The first medical study of a patient with dyslexia, then called "word blindness," is published.

Dyslexia and ADHD

People who suffer from dyslexia are also likely to have another disorder called attention deficit/hyperactivity disorder (ADHD). But even though they often go together, dyslexia and ADHD are separate disorders. While dyslexia is a language and reading disorder, ADHD creates problems with attention and behavior. Some research shows that the same brain areas are involved in both conditions.

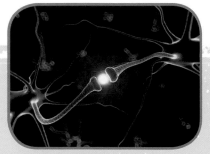

1925
A study shows that dyslexia is not related to brain damage.

1930s
Researchers develop new teaching methods for students struggling with dyslexia. These methods are still used today.

1960s
The first centers for studying and teaching children with dyslexia open in the United States and the United Kingdom.

35

Medications for Dyslexia?

Unfortunately, there are no medications for dyslexia. But because dyslexia and ADHD often occur together, some people assume that ADHD medication can help dyslexia as well. That doesn't seem to be the case. Some people on ADHD medication find that their dyslexia is easier to manage, but doctors believe that is because they are more able to focus and pay attention.

While drugs such as Adderall can help control ADHD symptoms, they are not effective in treating dyslexia.

Dyslexia Danger

One of the worst things about dyslexia is the way it can make a person feel. Before Joey understood his disorder, he felt stupid compared to the other kids. He worried that his teacher thought he was goofing off. It is important to diagnose dyslexia early so these feelings don't grow and create problems later on. Dyslexia treatment is most effective if it is started before a child begins to fall behind in school. Parents and teachers need to be on the lookout for children who are having a hard time reading.

CHAPTER 5

Myths and Facts

Even though scientists and doctors have learned a lot about dyslexia, many people still don't understand the condition. Some think dyslexia is a vision problem that causes people to see words and letters backward. Another common idea is that boys are more likely to be dyslexic than girls. However, neither of these things are true.

 Between 25 and 40 percent of children with dyslexia also have ADHD.

Understanding the Truth

The first thing to know is that dyslexia has nothing to do with intelligence. Some of history's brightest people may have struggled with this reading disorder. Among them are Alexander Graham Bell, a scientist and inventor who created the first telephone. Nobel Prize–winning physicist Albert Einstein is also believed to have had dyslexia. So is Thomas Edison, the inventor of the lightbulb, the motion-picture camera, and many other devices.

Albert Einstein's forgetfulness and difficulty learning new words as a child indicate that he may have been dyslexic.

No amount of studying can overcome dyslexia without additional help.

Another myth is that people with dyslexia can overcome the disorder by simply studying harder. Because dyslexia is based on a physical difference in the brain, studying harder will not help. It takes a special kind of teaching, and sometimes a bit of extra time to work on assignments, to help a person with dyslexia become a good reader and do well in school.

It is also a myth that dyslexia is a vision problem. Studies have shown that dyslexic people usually have normal vision. Reversing letters and words can be a sign of dyslexia, but many children without the disorder also do that. The belief that dyslexia mostly affects boys is also a myth. Researchers have found that girls are just as likely to suffer from the disorder.

Simple vision tests prove that dyslexia does not affect a person's eyesight.

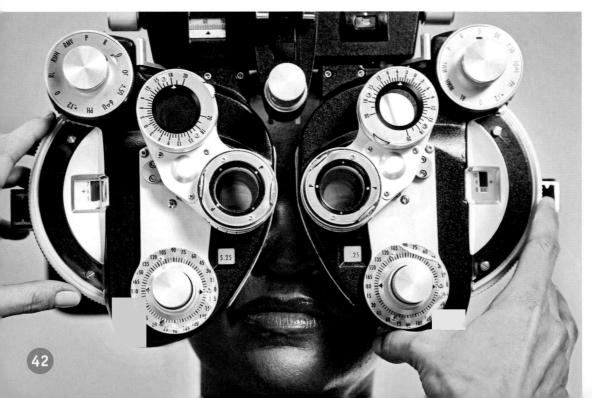

Even if you have dyslexia, you can learn to read and write, and you can enjoy books.

If you have been diagnosed with dyslexia, it is important to understand that it's not your fault. Your brain may be wired a bit differently, but that's one of the things that makes you special. Your dyslexia won't go away, but with the right kind of treatment, you can learn to be a good reader, enjoy reading, and do well in school and throughout your life. ★

True Statistics

Percent of Americans affected by dyslexia: 10 to 15

Percent of people with dyslexia who are receiving treatment: 5

Percent of children with learning disabilities who have dyslexia: About 80

Number of adults in the United States who are dyslexic: 30 million

Percent of people with poor reading skills who are likely to be dyslexic: 70 to 80

Did you find the truth?

T Many successful people have suffered from dyslexia.

F There are a number of medicines that are used to treat dyslexia.

Resources

Books

Esham, Barbara. *If You're So Smart, How Come You Can't Spell Mississippi?* Ocean City, MD: Mainstream Connections, 2014.

Moore-Mallinos, Jennifer. *It's Called Dyslexia.* Hauppauge, NY: Barron's Educational Series, 2007.

Robb, Diane Burton. *The Alphabet War: A Story About Dyslexia.* Morton Grove, IL: Albert Whitman & Co., 2004.

Visit this Scholastic Web site for more information on dyslexia:
★ www.factsfornow.scholastic.com
Enter the keyword **Dyslexia**

Important Words

corpus callosum (KOR-puhs kuh-LOW-sum) the band of tissue connecting the two brain hemispheres of higher mammals, including humans

diagnose (dye-ugh-NOHS) to determine what disease a patient has or what the cause of a problem is

disorder (dis-OR-dur) a physical or mental illness

genes (JEENZ) cellular material passed from parents to children that determines how you look and the way you grow

hemispheres (HEM-uh-sfeerz) the two halves of the brain

learning disability (LERN-ing dis-uh-BIL-uh-tee) a condition that interferes with a person's ability to learn basic academic skills

neurobiological (noo-roh-bye-uh-LAH-ji-kuhl) having to do with the function of the body, brain, and nervous system

phonemes (FOH-neemz) the smallest units of speech that can be used to make one word different from another word

phonemic awareness (fuh-NEE-mik uh-WAIR-niss) the understanding of speech sounds and how they make up words

spatial (SPAY-shuhl) relating to the way people perceive the positions of objects around them

Index

Page numbers in **bold** indicate illustrations.

About the Author

Ann O. Squire is a psychologist and an animal behaviorist. Before becoming a writer, she studied the behavior of rats, tropical fish in the Caribbean, and electric fish from central Africa. Her favorite part of being a writer is the chance to learn as much as she can about all sorts of topics. In addition to *Dyslexia* and books on other health topics, Dr. Squire has written about many different animals, from lemmings to leopards and cicadas to cheetahs. She lives in Asheville, North Carolina.